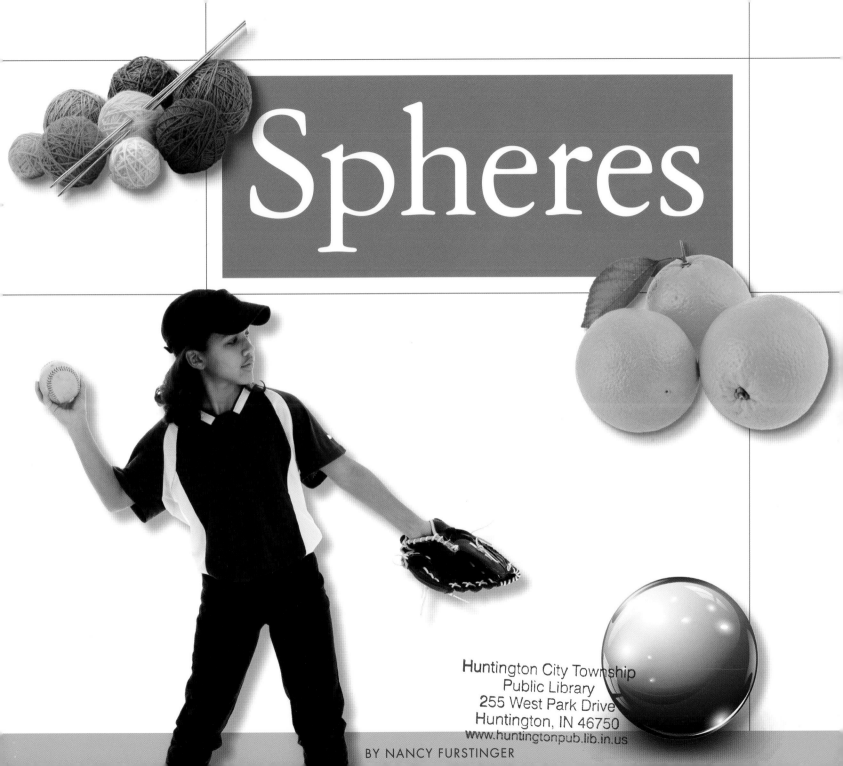

Spheres

BY NANCY FURSTINGER

Published by The Child's World®
1980 Lookout Drive • Mankato, MN 56003-1705
800-599-READ • www.childsworld.com

Acknowledgments
The Child's World®: Mary Berendes, Publishing Director
Red Line Editorial: Editorial direction
The Design Lab: Design

Photographs ©: Shutterstock Images, cover (top left),
cover (bottom right), 1 (top left), 1 (bottom right),
3 (left), 6, 9, 22, 23; Valzan/Shutterstock Images, cover
(top right), 1 (top right), 3 (right), 5; Rob Marmion/
Shutterstock Images, cover (bottom left), 1 (bottom left),
10; iStockphoto/Thinkstock, 4, 21; Cheryl Casey/
Shutterstock Images, 11, 15; Hemera/Thinkstock, 12;
Phelan M. Ebenhack/AP Images, 17; Jan Bussan/
Shutterstock Images, 18; Stockbyte/Thinkstock, 19

ISBN 9781623239862
LCCN 2013947245

Printed in the United States of America
Mankato, MN
November, 2013
PA02194

ABOUT THE AUTHOR

Award-winning author Nancy Furstinger enjoys searching for inspiring shapes in nature as she hikes with her big pooches. She is the author of more than 100 books.

CONTENTS

JUGGLING BALLS AND JUICE

Have you ever tried to juggle?

At a street festival, you spy a juggler. She juggles five balls higher and higher in the air. You get dizzy just watching her!

Next, you play a carnival game. You have three softballs to throw. You hit the target! You choose a large, fuzzy ball for your prize.

At a nearby booth, you order fresh-squeezed orange juice. You watch the bright, juicy oranges tumble into

the squeezing machine.
Did you notice how
the **shape** of the balls
matches the shape of the
oranges? Both of these
shapes are **spheres**.

Spheres are a lot of fun!

WHAT DOES A SPHERE LOOK LIKE?

Sphere shapes are all around us. Spheres have three **dimensions**. They aren't flat like circles. Circles and flat shapes have only two dimensions: length and width. Flat shapes are also called plane shapes or 2-D shapes.

Spheres and other shapes that have three dimensions are **3-D** shapes. 3-D shapes are also called solid shapes.

How can we identify a sphere? Look closely. A sphere is perfectly round, like a ball. This shape has no **edges** or corners.

A sphere has only one **surface**. It goes all around the sphere.

All points on the surface of the sphere are the same distance from the center.

A sphere has no edges or corners.

SPHERES AT PLAY

Now you can easily spot this 3-D shape. You'll see spheres everywhere you go.

You meet your friends at the playground. Some are playing a game of soccer. Others are practicing hitting softballs. One is dribbling a basketball. Two are tossing a beach ball in the pool. All of these balls are shaped like spheres. Can you think of a ball that is not shaped like a sphere?

Your brother is playing jacks. He bounces a rubber ball, picks up jacks, and catches the ball before it

Use the large shooter to knock other marbles out of the ring.

bounces again. When he's bored, he can switch to a game of marbles. Your sister is blowing soap bubbles. Each bubble has colors that swirl and shimmer. What other games use sphere shapes?

Old-Time Games

Jacks was once called knucklebones because it was played with sheep bones 2,000 years ago. Today, this game of skill is played with pointy metal jacks and a bouncing ball. The game of marbles has been popular for 3,000 years. Shooter and playing marbles were made of clay, stone, or marble. Today, kids play with a rainbow of glass marbles.

How many types of fruit that are spheres can you count in this picture?

SPHERES WE EAT

Some spheres are juicy! When you visit the supermarket, explore the produce section. Many fruits have this 3-D shape. Squeeze oranges, tangerines, and grapefruits into juices. Watch a grown-up slice cantaloupe and honeydew melons. Pop blueberries in your mouth.

Many vegetables are also shaped like spheres. Shell a pod of green peas. Shred a head of cabbage. Top a salad with cherry tomatoes.

SWEET SPHERES

Some spheres taste sweet. Chocolate candy comes wrapped in foil, covered in nuts, or inside a shiny coat of color. When you bite into it, what do you find inside? The chocolate might be hiding a caramel, marshmallow, or cherry center.

Lick a lemon lollipop and watch your tongue turn yellow. Set your mouth on fire with fireballs. Can giant jawbreakers really break your jaws? Chew bubble gum balls. Then blow a big round bubble.

How big of a bubble can you blow?

Largest Bubble Gum Bubble Blown

According to Guinness World Records, a man blew the world's biggest bubble gum bubble without using his hands in 2004. The bubble measured 20 inches (50.8 cm) in **diameter**. That's the size of a beach ball!

Huntington City Township Public Library
255 West Park Drive
Huntington, IN 46750
www.huntingtonpub.lib.in.us

BUILDING SPHERES

Some buildings are shaped like spheres. Perhaps
the most famous is Spaceship Earth at Walt Disney
World's Epcot Center. Riders spiral up 18 stories on a
time-machine adventure. This 16-million-pound
(7 million kg) sphere looks like a giant silver
golf ball!

Another sphere has found a second life in
Canada. The Montreal Biosphere dome starred in
that city's 1967 World Fair. Today this steel sphere
houses a museum.

Spaceship Earth in Walt Disney World is shaped like a sphere.

SPHERES FOR ALL SEASONS

Spheres appear in every season. In the winter, we shake snow globes and watch flakes swirl around the scenes inside. Outside, we shape snow into spheres. Stack up three to make a snowman.

In the spring, flowers like allium and

fluffy white dandelions grow in the shape of a sphere. Some people trim their shrubs into sphere shapes.

In the summer, we go to the beach. Play catch with a giant beach ball. On a pebbly beach, look for a stone that is perfectly round. Can you find one?

In the fall, we trick-or-treat on Halloween. We hope to bring home mounds of round candy. Later, we shape popcorn balls. What a yummy snack!

A beach ball is great for a game of catch.

SPHERES IN SPACE

Did you know our planet Earth is a huge sphere? Our planet has been described as a "blue marble." It appears blue because most of Earth is covered with water. Look at a globe. You can see that 70 percent of Earth's surface is covered in water.

The eight planets in our solar system are all shaped like spheres. **Gravity** causes planets to form this shape. Every point on the planet's surface is pulled evenly toward the center. The result is a sphere shape.

Search for sphere shapes wherever you go. You can find these 3-D shapes everywhere, here on Earth and out of this world!

Earth is a sphere, and so are the other planets.

HANDS-ON ACTIVITY: BUBBLE FUN

Mix up this homemade bubble solution. Then wave the wand and watch your bubbles take flight!

Materials

- 2-1/2 quarts water
- 1/2 cup light corn syrup
- 1 cup clear liquid dish detergent
- food coloring
- spoon
- pail
- clothes hanger
- pliers
- cotton twine or yarn
- pie tin

Directions

1. Stir together the water and corn syrup in a pail. Add the liquid dish detergent and gently stir. You can make colored bubbles by adding a few drops of food coloring.
2. Make a wand. Have an adult help you unravel the hanger using pliers. Bend one end of the wire into a loop shape. Cover this shape with the twine or yarn. Bend the other end into a handle.
3. Pour the soap bubble solution into the pie tin.
4. Dip the loop end of the wand into the solution. Wave the wand and watch your soap bubbles soar!

GLOSSARY

diameter (dye-AM-i-tur): The diameter is a straight line running from one side of a circle through the center to the other side. Measure the diameter of a sphere through its center.

dimensions (duh-MEN-shuns): Dimensions are the length, width, or height of an object. A sphere's height is one of its dimensions.

edges (EJ-uhs): Edges are the lines where a surface begins or ends. A sphere has no edges.

gravity (GRAV-i-tee): Gravity is the force that pulls objects toward the center of Earth and other stars and planets. The pull of gravity shapes planets into spheres.

spheres (SFEER): Spheres are 3-D shapes that are rounded like a globe. Spheres have no edges or corners.

surface (SUR-fis): A surface is the flat or curved border of a 3-D shape. A sphere is a single curved surface.

3-D (THREE-DEE): A 3-D shape has three dimensions, length, width, and height. A 3-D shape is not flat.

BOOKS

Brocket, Jane. *Circles, Stars, and Squares*. Minneapolis: Millbrook Press, 2013.

Cohen, Marina. *My Path to Math: 3-D Shapes*. New York: Crabtree Publishing Company, 2011.

Hoban, Tana. *Cubes, Cones, Cylinders, & Spheres*. New York: Greenwillow Books, 2000.

WEB SITES

Visit our Web site for links about Spheres: *childsworld.com/links*

Note to Parents, Teachers, and Librarians:
We routinely verify our Web links to make sure they are safe and active sites.
So encourage your readers to check them out!

INDEX